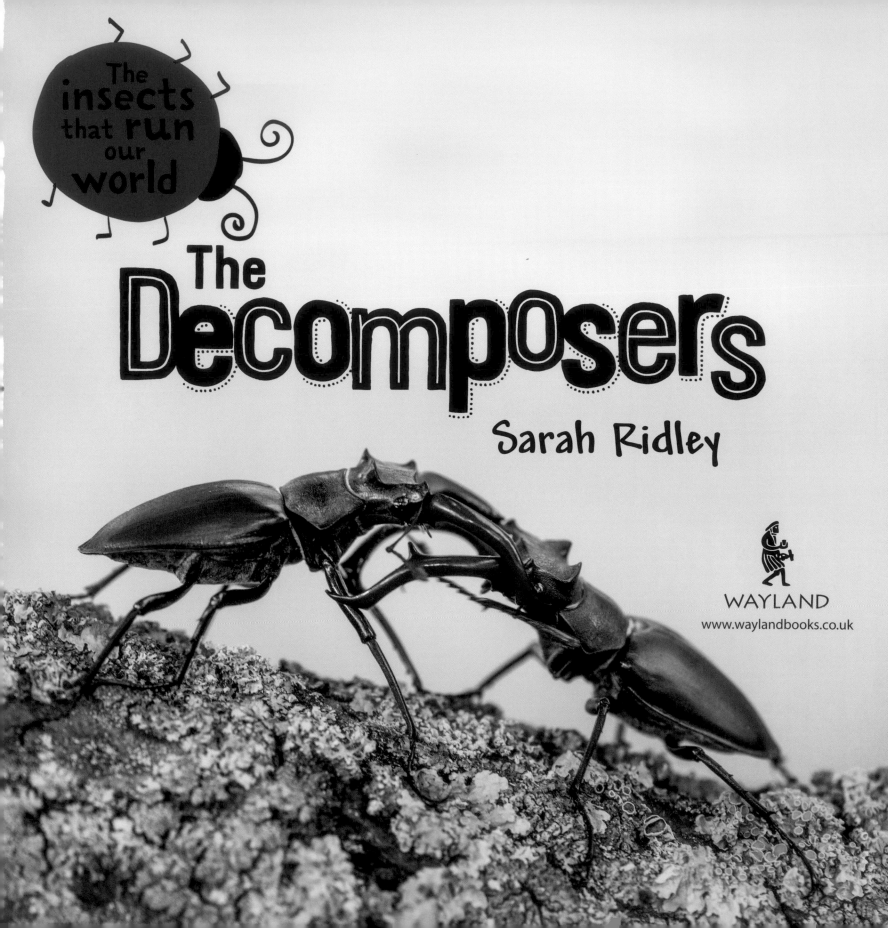

The insects that **run** our **world**

The Decomposers

Sarah Ridley

WAYLAND
www.waylandbooks.co.uk

First published in Great Britain in 2021
by Wayland

Copyright © Hodder and Stoughton, 2021

Editor: Sarah Peutrill
Designer: Lisa Peacock
Consultant: Buglife, the Invertebrate Conservation Trust

HB ISBN: 978 1 5263 1403 1
PB ISBN: 978 1 5263 1404 8

Printed and bound in China

Wayland, an imprint of
Hachette Children's Group
Part of Hodder and Stoughton
Carmelite House
50 Victoria Embankment
London EC4Y 0DZ
An Hachette UK Company

www.hachette.co.uk
www.hachettechildrens.co.uk

Picture credits:
Dreamstime: Digitalimagined 8r. Istock: Eliane29 5t;
Volodymyr Kyrylyuk 7t; Evgeny Meinikov cover, 1;
milehightraveler 5b. Nature Picture Library: Simon
Colmer 22; Mark Moffet 11; Dietmar Nill 10; Constantinos
Petrinos 8l; Premaphotos 15, 17; Marie Read 21; Nick Upton
16; Visuals Unlimited 23t; Steffan Widstrand 3, 12.
Shutterstock: Dan Bagur 2, 14; R.Classen 4b; Karel Gallas
19c; Gil.K 9; Jim Lambert 20b; Henrik Larsson 18t, 18b,
19tr, 20t, 23b; Bernatskaia Oksana 4tr; Cristina Romero
Palma 4tl; Michael Potter11 13; Martina Unbehauen 6;
Yxowert 7b.

Every attempt has been made to clear copyright.
Should there be any inadvertent omission please apply
to the publisher for rectification.

Blow flies

Contents

The decomposers

What is special about these insects?

Green bottle fly

Ants

Dung beetle

They are decomposers. They love eating dead stuff, poo and food scraps, helping to break them down to recycle the goodness locked up inside.

When someone dropped this crust on the ground, ants found it. Ants take tiny bits of the food back to their nest to eat.

On the forest floor in Madagascar, hissing cockroaches eat dead plants or fruit.

Without insect decomposers, the Earth would be in trouble.

What do decomposers do?

Insect decomposers eat dead plants and animals, poo and food waste, helping to break it down into tiny pieces.

These rose chafer beetle grubs are munching on dead plants and vegetable scraps in a compost heap.

Insects are not the only decomposers. Bacteria, fungi and other minibeasts, such as woodlice and worms, are all decomposers.

Many sorts of beetle grubs, also called larvae, help to release the goodness in dead plants so that it can be used again. The dead plants give them the energy to live, grow and become adult beetles.

When the compost is ready, gardeners mix it into soil to help plants grow well.

The grubs shown on the opposite page will change into beautiful rose chafer beetles, like this one.

Cleaning up the mess

Without decomposers, dead plants and animals would pile up everywhere. Decomposers act like caretakers of our world, cleaning up dead stuff.

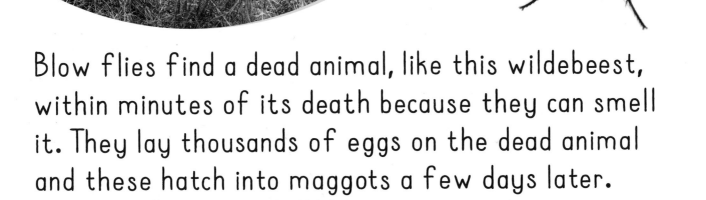

Blow flies find a dead animal, like this wildebeest, within minutes of its death because they can smell it. They lay thousands of eggs on the dead animal and these hatch into maggots a few days later.

8

The maggots feast until they are ready to turn into adult flies two to three weeks later. Gradually the dead animal is eaten up by maggots and other animals until all that remains are its bones.

It will take about seven years for the bones of this wildebeest to crumble away.

Decomposers are nature's recyclers, reusing or releasing the good things locked up in dead animals and plants.

Burying beetles

The smell of this dead vole attracted a sexton beetle, also called a burying beetle. Soon others will arrive. Working in pairs or with a group, they will remove soil from under the vole to bury it.

After sexton beetles have buried a dead animal, the female beetle lays her eggs close to the body. When the larvae hatch, they feed on the dead body.

Some types of sexton beetle even feed tiny bits to their young during their first days of life.

The beetle larvae are using important nutrients in the dead body to help them grow. This way, the nutrients are not lost.

Rolling away the poo

Without insect decomposers, wild animal poo would pile up on the ground. Dung beetles can carry away a pile of poo in a few hours if enough beetles are attracted to the poo.

These dung beetles are gathering dung in South Africa. Dung beetles live across the world.

These dung beetles work together to roll a poo ball away. They will bury it, lay an egg in it and the dung ball will become home and food for their baby beetle.

Other dung beetles make tunnels and fill it with bits of dung to feed their young or lay their eggs in the dung pile itself.

13

Flies like poo too

Blow flies and houseflies like to eat animal poo. When the fly lands on a poo it is sick on it, to help make the food into soup. Now the fly can suck up the soup using its special mouth.

Flies feed on animal poo.

Meanwhile, dung flies see cowpats as a perfect place to find a mate and lay their eggs. Their maggots hatch after one or two days, burrow into the cowpat and eat it until they are ready to become adults.

Dung flies, dung beetles and their babies help break down a cowpat in seven to twenty weeks.

Without dung beetles and dung flies, dung would lie on the ground for much, much longer and stop plants from growing.

15

Seaside and forest flies

After a high tide, seaweed is left on beaches around the coast. It does not break down easily. Luckily, kelp flies love eating rotting seaweed, as do their young.

The flat body of a kelp fly helps it squeeze through gaps in a pile of seaweed. This one is resting on a shell.

In the rainforests of Central and South America, timber fly larvae help recycle dead and dying trees. If there are lots of larvae inside one tree, their munching can be heard from several metres away!

Like all decomposers, these flies are top recyclers, breaking down dead plants into tiny bits that can be used again by other living things.

Adult timber flies can be 8 cm long, making them some of the largest flies in the world.

17

Dead wood and beetle babies

It is not just timber flies that lay their eggs in trees. They can be the perfect place for some beetle mothers to lay their eggs. There is plenty of food and shelter for the larvae when they hatch.

This longhorn beetle larva will tunnel through a dead pine tree for about three years before it turns into ...

... an adult longhorn beetle.

Stag beetle mothers lay their eggs in soil close to rotting wood. The larvae feed on the wood for between three and seven years before they turn into magnificent adult beetles.

Male stag beetle

The adult great capricorn beetle lives for a few weeks but spends between three and five years as a larva inside a dead tree.

It can take from thirty to hundreds of years for a dead tree to disappear in nature.

19

Decomposers in trouble

Sadly, there are far fewer insects on Earth than there were fifty years ago. This is because there are fewer places where they can live, they are being killed by pesticides and they struggle with climate change.

Pesticides are fed to cows and horses and some end up in their dung, harming or killing the beetles that eat dung.

We are covering more and more land with buildings and roads, leaving little space for wildlife.

The beetle larva in this woodpecker's beak was a decomposer and is about to become the next meal for its chicks.

All living things on Earth, including insects, play their part in keeping our planet healthy. They are all important.

Helping the decomposers

Insect decomposers help to run our world. Here are a few ways that we can help these important insects.

In the garden, ask your family to be less tidy! Choose a shady spot, dig a shallow hole and stack up some logs to attract beetles. Do not disturb the log pile as some beetle larvae take years to become adults.

Don't use pesticides on the garden. These chemicals kill both insect pests and insects that help garden plants grow.

Create an open compost heap for uncooked fruit and vegetable scraps, twigs, grass cuttings and leaves to attract beetles and other minibeasts.

Ask your parents to support your local wildlife charity. They care for wild spaces and wildlife, including insects. This Swedish forest provides homes for lots of insect decomposers because trees are left to rot down slowly when they die.

23

Glossary

bacteria The simplest and smallest forms of life.

climate change A change in the normal weather around the world.

compost A mixture of decomposed plant material and food scraps.

decomposer A living thing that helps dead stuff to decompose (rot), breaking it down into tiny bits.

fungi Living things that feed on dead material, helping it to decompose.

green bottle fly A type of blow fly.

insect An animal with six legs and a body divided into three parts.

larva Insect young.

maggot The young of a fly. It looks like a short worm.

nutrient A substance that helps plants and animals to live and grow.

pesticide A chemical liquid or powder used to kill harmful insects or weeds.

recycle Release and/or reuse the nutrients in dead material or waste material.

timber Wood used for making things.

Index